Jane Leadbetter

Messy Easter

Three Complete Sessions and a Treasure Trove of Ideas for Lent, Holy Week, and Easter

IVP Books

An imprint of InterVarsity Press
Downers Grove, Illinois

InterVarsity Press
P.O. Box 1400, Downers Grove, IL 60515-1426
ivpress.com
email@ivpress.com

InterVarsity Press® is the book-publishing division of InterVarsity Christian Fellowship/USA®, a movement of students and faculty active on campus at hundreds of universities, colleges, and schools of nursing in the United States of America, and a member movement of the International Fellowship of Evangelical Students. For information about local and regional activities, visit intervarsity.org.

All Scripture quotations, unless otherwise indicated, are taken from The Holy Bible, New International Version®, NIV®. Copyright © 1973, 1978, 1984, 2011 by Biblica, Inc.™ Used by permission of Zondervan. All rights reserved worldwide. www.zondervan.com. The "NIV" and "New International Version" are trademarks registered in the United States Patent and Trademark Office by Biblica, Inc.™

Cover design: Cindy Kiple
Images: jellybeans: © mayakova/iStockphoto
    Easter eggs photo: Nathan Baker-Lutz
    green grass photo: Nathan Baker-Lutz
    white wooden wall: © eugenesergeev/iStockphoto
    ink splashes: © voinSveta/iStockphoto
    decorated Easter eggs: Nathan Baker-Lutz
    popsicle stick cross: Nathan Baker-Lutz

ISBN 978-0-8308-4140-0 (print)
ISBN 978-0-8308-8892-4 (digital)

Printed in the United States of America ♾

InterVarsity Press is committed to ecological stewardship and to the conservation of natural resources in all our operations. This book was printed using sustainably sourced paper.

Library of Congress Cataloging-in-Publication Data
A catalog record for this book is available from the Library of Congress.

P 37 36 35 34 33 32 31 30 29 28 27 26 25 24 23 22 21 20 19 18 17 16 15 14 13 12 11 10 9 8 7 6 5 4 3 2 1

Y 50 49 48 47 46 45 44 43 42 41 40 39 38 37 36 35 34 33 32 31 30 29 28 27 26 25 24 23 22 21 20 19 18 17

For all of my crafty friends

Contents

Planning Grid for Messy Church

Theme: _____ Date: _____

Crafts	Preparation	Craft Leader	Notes

Available as a download from www.messychurch.org.uk/resource/messy-church-planning-grid.

Introduction

Happy Easter!

The timing of Easter may change each year, but when it comes, hurrah! Easter is one of the three most important times in the Christian church calendar, along with Christmas and Pentecost. We have a time to prepare for it: Lent. We have a time of exceptional events to explore on the way: Holy Week. Then we arrive at one of the most joyous and great celebrations of the year: Easter Sunday!

The season of Lent and Easter gathers together thoughts about preparation, abstinence, repentance, reflection, self-sacrifice, death, resurrection, forgiveness, hope, assurance, and celebration. Easter is the celebration of Christ's resurrection from the dead. As it is the oldest and most important festival of the Christian church, it also includes many traditions, depending on where in the world you live.

Your Messy Church, if monthly, could fall at any time between the beginning of Lent and Easter Sunday. You may wish to pack the whole story into two hours, select some special themes, or cover just part of the journey to Easter and continue it next year. However you offer Easter to your community, please use this book as a grab bag of choices. It is important that we find as many ways as we can to help families engage with the real story of Easter.

This book explores the desert in Lent, uncovers the key events of Holy Week, and helps you to experience the surprise of Easter morning. The three sessions invite all ages to discover the elements of the Easter story through many methods and styles of creativity, using many different art media and skills. Everyone learns in different ways, so there is a wide variety of ideas for those who enjoy activity-based learning.

In addition to the three main sessions, there is an Easter Extras section with additional ideas. It is less detailed but gives examples of alternative crafts and activities to use at any Easter occasion.

Messy Church offers an abundance of opportunities to share the Easter story with the community. We hear great stories of Messy Churches where hundreds of people of all ages gather to open up the Easter story and eat hot cross buns together. Some Messy Churches join with their local school to explore the Easter journey, and some use the Saturday between Good Friday and Easter Sunday, a day of waiting, to shout out the message that Jesus is alive. Thank you, Messy Churches everywhere, for your wonderful all-age ministry in your local communities. Enjoy the mess! And not an Easter bunny in sight . . .

Lent Messy Church

- **Theme:** Preparing for Easter.

- **Biblical story:** Jesus in the wilderness for forty days of preparation for his ministry, facing temptations from the devil.

- **Equipping today's families:** By discovering what happened to Jesus in the desert, we can find God in our own desert times. God wants to build endurance into our lives, to strengthen us as we follow him. The season of Lent invites us on a journey of hope.

The Bible passages for this story are Matthew 4:1–11; Mark 1:12–13; and Luke 4:1–13.

Crafts

Desert cactus

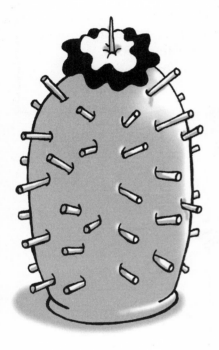

You will need:

Two cups flour, two cups water, one cup salt, four tablespoons cream of tartar, two tablespoons oil, green food coloring, toothpicks or uncooked spaghetti, small pieces of brightly colored tissue paper, and printouts of various cactus shapes.

How to

In advance of the session, make play dough by mixing the flour, water, salt, cream of tartar, and oil in a microwave-safe bowl. Add your desired amount of food coloring. Stir well and place in a microwave. Heat for three minutes on high power. Stir again and heat for another three minutes. Allow the dough to cool, then knead it. Place in an airtight tin or use plastic wrap.

Take a small ball of play dough and create any cactus shape. Insert broken pieces of spaghetti or toothpicks into the cactus for the spines. Make one tissue paper flower and attach it to the cactus with a toothpick.

Talk about how the desert is a dry and barren place, but the cactus plant can grow very long roots and store up moisture. It can fight off hungry animals by growing sharp spines, and some cacti display beautiful flowers. Just as a cactus stores up water to give it strength, we need Jesus to be the source of our strength. Jesus said, "Everyone who drinks this water will be thirsty again, but whoever drinks the water I give them will never thirst. Indeed, the water I give them will become in them a spring of water welling up to eternal life" (John 4:13–14).

Lenten cross puzzle

You will need:

Pieces of medium rough sandpaper; scissors; cross template (page 88); and purple, gray, or dark blue crayons.

How to

Trace the cross template on the reverse side of a piece of sandpaper. Cut out the cross shape with scissors. On the rough side of the sandpaper, make patterns on the cross with crayons.
To create a jigsaw puzzle, cut the cross into six pieces.

Talk about how the color purple symbolizes pain and suffering and is used by many churches during the season of Lent. Other colors used are red, dark blue, and gray. Touch the rough texture of the sandpaper. Jesus had a hard time in the desert, feeling lonely, hungry, and thirsty, but he showed how he needed only the bread of heaven, the word of God, to survive.

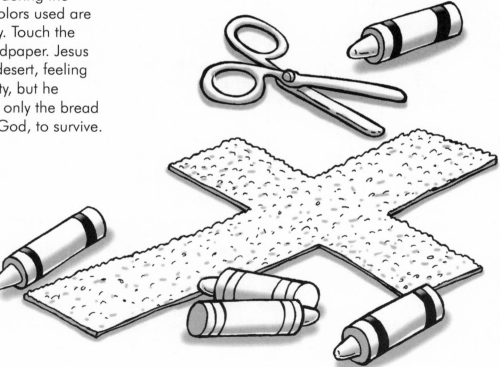

Sackcloth bags

You will need:

Pieces of sackcloth or rough material, yarn, needles, purple markers, and puzzle pieces from previous activity.

Talk about how sackcloth is another symbol of Lent. Along with ashes, it symbolizes mourning, mortality, and penance. Sackcloth was worn at sad times by many people in the Bible, including Jacob, David, Daniel, and the Ninevites after they heard Jonah's message.

How to

Cut a piece of sackcloth approximately fifteen inches by six inches. Fold it in half and sew up each side with yarn, leaving the top open. Using the markers, decorate the bag with purple crosses.

Place your jigsaw pieces inside the sackcloth bag and remove just one piece each week during Lent. Gradually form the shape of the cross by piecing together the puzzle, somewhere in your home, as a reminder of Jesus' forty days in the wilderness and the forty days of Lent. The sandpaper will also remind you of Jesus in the desert.

11

Snakes in the sand

You will need:

Ready-made fondant icing, selection of food coloring, powdered sugar, thin paintbrushes, edible candy for eyes, red sugar paste, brown sugar (optional), and paper plates.

How to

Roll out a ball of icing to form a snake shape and place it on a paper plate. Mix together some food coloring in small bowls and paint snakeskin markings on the icing. Finish with edible candy eyes (use a powdered sugar and water paste to glue together) and a sugar paste tongue. Sprinkle powdered sugar or brown sugar on the plate to represent the sandy desert.

Talk about how snakes are featured throughout the Bible. In the deserts of the Bible, the snakes would have been able to adapt to the hot days and cold nights, eating and drinking only every couple of days. Jesus would have been vulnerable to these "wild beasts" in the desert.

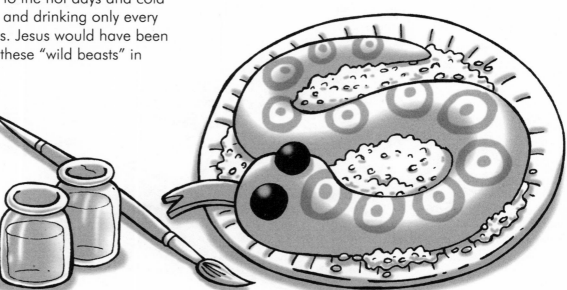

Dangerous words

You will need:

Scrabble boards and letters (or letter tiles from another word-based board game), paper, and markers.

Talk about spending long hot days and cold nights with no food or drink. What kind of animals would there be in the desert? How dangerous would it be? Who could you talk to? What would you do in an emergency? How would you feel for the first ten days? Would you feel any different after forty days?

How to

Think about how Jesus would have felt in the desert for forty days and nights, then think of some words to describe how he was feeling. Try to link the words together using the Scrabble letters, or use markers on large pieces of paper to create a similar crossword.

Wilderness sand pits

You will need:

Various kiddie pools, depending on space available, sand, stones, bare branches, dead or dried plants, paper, markers, scissors, toy buckets and spades, and other sand toys.

How to

Place the kiddie pools, filled with sand, next to each other. Make sure you have more than one, as one will be for free play and the other(s) will be used to create a desert. Use the stones and dried materials to make your desert, including drawings of animals, cacti, bones, or whatever you like. Place the sand toys in another kiddie pool for free play.

Talk about how hot the desert is and what would survive in the heat. What could you build a shelter with? How long can we survive without water or food? Would Jesus have stayed in one place for forty days and nights or moved around? What happens in the desert when it rains? Have you ever been lost in a wilderness?

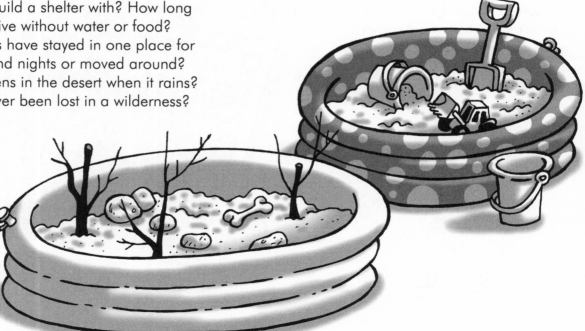

Ash Wednesday artists

You will need:

Roll of white paper, roll of black paper, colored chalk, white chalk, charcoal pencils/sticks, pastel crayons, masking tape, and picture of person with ash cross.

Talk about how Lent begins on Ash Wednesday, when some churches offer their congregations an ash cross marked on their forehead as a sign of repentance and commitment. The ash is made by burning the previous year's palm crosses and is mixed with a little water or oil to make a paste.

How to

Create an artist's wall with alternating black and white paper stripes. Using masking tape, stick it either on a wall, cabinet, or flat on the floor. In the center, place a picture of someone who has received an ash cross on their forehead, with a short explanation in large text. Invite all ages to draw a cross using any of the media provided. As you draw a cross, think about how you might want to say "sorry" to God.

Pretzel prayers

You will need:

Pretzels, ribbon, strong paper or cardstock, hole punch, crazy cut scissors, copies of the story of the pretzel (page 17), and shoelaces.

How to

Use the crazy cut scissors to cut a small square of cardstock. Punch a hole in the square and write a prayer on it, thanking God for his love. Tie the prayer to a pretzel with enough loose ribbon to enable it to hang up. Hang your pretzel prayer near your front door at home. Every time you leave your home, it will remind you that God is close to you wherever you go, wrapping his arms around you with love.

Use the shoelace to practice making a pretzel shape on the craft table.

Talk about the story of the pretzel and look at the pretzel shape. It is believed to represent arms crossed in prayer because in the days of the early church, people crossed their arms across their chest for prayer. Taste a pretzel and try to guess what it is made of. Lent is a time of fasting—giving something up for forty days—as well as of prayer. Pretzels are made from flour and water and have been popular Lenten fasting food for years.

The story of the pretzel

Pretzels are not mentioned in the Bible and neither is Lent, but as traditions they go back a long time. There are various stories about how they came about, and it is unclear in exactly which year or which European country pretzels originated. Here is one story.

In about AD 610, a monk was baking unleavened bread for Lent in his kitchen. Through the window he could see children praying. He decided to make treats for the children as a reward for reciting their prayers, so he used up the leftover pieces of dough to create strips folded like the arms of a person praying. The shapes were called *pretiola*, Latin for "little reward," from which the word *pretzel* has been derived. Since then, pretzels have remained a popular Lenten food, and there are lots of different shapes and recipes.

Handy angels

You will need:

White paper, yellow and blue paint, paper plates, and glitter.

How to

Squirt some yellow paint on to two paper plates and some blue paint on to two more plates. Place one hand in each of the yellow paints and make two handprints on the white paper, side by side, to make angel's wings. Wash your hands and then place both hands in the blue paint. Make one handprint at the center of the two wings to make a body shape, splaying out the thumb to the side as an arm. Then place a second handprint on top of the first one, again splaying out the thumb to the side, making another arm.

Rotate the paper 180 degrees and you will see angel wings and a body. Use a finger to paint a head and halo. Add some glitter to the halo. Add facial features with anything handy or with a marker when the paint is dry.

Talk about how Jesus was led by the Holy Spirit into the desert to be tempted by the devil. He overcame wild beasts and the devil, and angels cared for him. Angels helped Jesus to endure his suffering. "Then the devil left him, and angels came and attended him" (Matthew 4:11).

Survival trail

You will need:

Ten pieces of cardstock or paper with the following pictures of items needed for survival, plus alphabet letters: water (Y), tent (I), first aid kit (R), sunscreen (H), bar of chocolate (P), map (L), blanket (I), hat (O), knife (S), box of matches (T); trail leaflets that include the list of ten items, with a blank space alongside each item; and selection of suitable small prizes.

Talk about what you would take with you if you could prepare a backpack of items to survive forty days in the desert. Jesus looked physically unprepared, but just before entering the desert he had been baptized and was filled with the Holy Spirit. He endured wild beasts, extreme weather, and testing from the devil without any food or comforts, but gained all the strength he needed from God.

How to

Stick the ten pieces of cardstock in various obvious places around your space at a suitable height for all ages to reach. At the activity table, issue a trail leaflet and a pencil per group. Invite the group to hunt for pictures of all ten items listed on their leaflet. They must enter, on the leaflet, the letter they discover next to each survival item. On completion, they will return to the activity table and unscramble the letters in order to answer the question: How did Jesus survive the desert?

If they find the answer HOLY SPIRIT, award them a suitable small prize, preferably angel-related: angel cake, angel halo (doughnut), chocolate or candy in a small angel gift bag, or an ice cream cone with angel wafer "wings." Be creative!

19

Celebration

Get ready

As people enter the worship space, play a slide show of pictures of the crafts and activities everyone has been doing. Play powerful music with a menacing theme. Explain that the crafts were chosen to help us to think about the six weeks of Lent and how Jesus was in the wilderness for forty days and nights. What happened to Jesus during this time?

If you like to use props during your storytelling, have ready some stones, an A-frame set of ladders, a photo of the world, and a sword. Invite all ages to raise their arm like a sword whenever you raise your sword and shout out loud, **"Jesus is the Son of God!"**

Go

Close your eyes for a moment. Try to picture what you think Jesus looks like. There are no right or wrong answers. I wonder if he looks happy and smiling or tired and sad. Is he long-haired with a beard, or messy-haired with a halo? Or is he a baby in a manger? Okay, open your eyes!

Well, Jesus was around thirty years old when he asked John the Baptist to baptize him. So picture the scene. There were the cool waters of the Jordan River, crowds of people who wanted to be baptized, and there was Jesus telling John that now was the time. John wasn't sure, but he baptized Jesus in the Jordan River anyway, and as Jesus came out of the water, the sky opened up and a bright light shone down on him. The Spirit of God came down like a dove and landed on Jesus. Then a voice from above said, "This is my Son. I love him and I am pleased with him."

Close your eyes again. Can you see Jesus now? How does he look this time?

What did God's voice say? "This is my Son." (*Raise your sword.*) **Jesus is the Son of God!**

Open your eyes! Jesus is now being led by the Holy Spirit into a desert. He had just heard God say how pleased he was with him, and now suddenly he is all alone in a dangerous place. Jesus has no food and goes hungry for forty days and nights. During this time the devil tempts him and challenges him about being the Son of God. The devil often tempts us when we are tired and hungry, sad, or feeling weak.

The temptations are a bit like when you receive ads in the mail or phone calls pestering you to change from one electricity or gas company to another where they promise you a better financial deal; or like when a mobile phone company tempts you to change provider and receive more apps and phone options for less money. The devil would love it if Jesus decided to move from his "provider," God, and work for the devil instead.

Jesus is facing the biggest challenge ever—and remember that Jesus is a man, fully human. He has to make important decisions every step of the way.

First, the devil tried to tempt Jesus by asking him to change some stones into bread. *(Show the stones.)* Now we know that Jesus could turn water into wine and multiply fish and bread loaves because we read about it in other Bible stories. But here Jesus responds by quoting the word of God showing how he trusts only God—because *(raise your sword)* **Jesus is the Son of God!**

Second, the devil took Jesus to the top of the temple in the holy city, Jerusalem, and asked him to throw himself down and let the angels catch him. The devil even quoted from Psalm 91 in the Bible, but Jesus also quoted from the Bible—a verse about not putting God to the test. *(Raise your sword.)* **Jesus is the Son of God!**

Third, the devil took Jesus to a high mountain and showed him all the kingdoms of the world. He offered it all to Jesus if Jesus would bow down and worship him. But how could the devil offer the world when it doesn't belong to him? It belongs to God! Jesus answered that we should worship only God. *(Raise your sword.)* **Jesus is the Son of God!**

Then the devil left and the angels came to care for Jesus. Jesus faced every temptation, but he resisted. He did not sin and give in. Now he was ready to work hard for around three and a half years, telling everyone about God his Father. *(Raise your sword.)* **Jesus is the Son of God!**

Remote control prayer

Give copies of the TV remote control template (page 89) to everyone. Then lead everyone in prayer:

The word "remote" can mean far away, distant, secluded, or faint. Jesus was far away and secluded when he was in the desert for forty days. Look at the buttons on your remote control for the desert. There are forty buttons, one for each day of Lent. There are other familiar buttons too.

Press button number 1 and pray with me.

> Thank you, Lord, for Ash Wednesday, the first day of Lent. We think of the ashes, which remind us how we are sorry for not always being close to you, and the dust of the desert, where Jesus suffered for forty days.

Now press the "fast forward" button.

> Help us, Lord, to think about the fasting in our lives, the things we will give up through Lent. Help us to declutter our lives as we grow to know you better.

Press buttons one through forty (as quickly as you can).

> We think about how you suffered in the desert and stood strong against the devil. Help us to keep strong in our love for God.

Press the "Guide" button.

Thank you for the Holy Spirit, who came to you on your baptism day, watched over you in the desert, and guides each of us every day.

Press the "Exit" button.

Because you are the Son of God, you invite each one of us to walk beside you in love and trust. Thank you, Lord, for resisting the devil. Help us to say "no" in times of weakness. Thank you for being in control. Amen.

Finish with the Messy Grace:

May the grace of our Lord Jesus Christ (*hold out your hands as if expecting a gift*)
And the love of God (*put your hands on your heart*)
And the fellowship of the Holy Spirit (*hold hands*)
Be with us all now and for ever. Amen! (*raise hands together on the word "Amen"*)

Cards to put on the meal table

- What did you like best about Messy Church today?
- If you could choose just one thing to take into the desert with you, what would it be?
- Have you ever been tempted and found it hard to resist?
- How do you think the angels cared for Jesus after his forty days in the desert?
- If Jesus was eating with you now, what would you ask him about his time in the desert?

Take-home ideas

- **Ash alms jar:** Choose an empty glass jar with a lid to decorate in gray, purple, or dark colors using glass paints or tissue paper. Make a coin-sized slit in the lid. Use the jar to collect coins for a needy cause during Lent.

- **Declutter:** Simplify your life by sorting and clearing unwanted and unused items in your home. They could be clothes, books, toys, or everything in the shed. Give some away to good causes.

- **Fast food fasting:** Avoid the junk food and takeaway options. Simplify your diet with healthy recipes and less rich food. What difference will this make to your well-being in six weeks?

Forty Messy Lent family challenges and activities

1. Make an ash alms jar and decide which charity you will collect coins for during Lent.

2. Think about what you could give up during Lent to enable you to redirect your money to the alms jar.

3. Decorate a notebook to make a Lent family journal. Chat together each evening and write about how you feel; thank God for something and pray for someone else.

4. Messy moaning: add a coin to the alms jar every time you complain about something.

5. Try a sugarless Saturday. You'll be surprised how much of what we eat contains sugar.

6. Choose a Bible story to read together.

7. The Western church doesn't count Sundays in the forty days of Lent. Take the opportunity to spend quality time together as a family and enjoy your Sundays.

8. Take it in turns and have each member of the family choose one story from the daily news and record it in the Lent family journal for prayer.

9. Keep a Bible and a book of Bible stories on top of the coffee table all through Lent.

10. Declutter your kitchen cupboards. Check "use by" dates on food items. Which cookbooks have you never used? How can you recycle those books?

11. Look at your remaining cookbooks together and give each other a health check by choosing healthy options more regularly. Create a family recipe binder of favorites.

12. Celebrate the parents or parental figures in your life. Prepare a loving day for them and particularly think about people who do not have a parent.

13. Experience a "turn off" day with your computers, TV, radio, phones, tablets, iPods, and so on. How difficult is it to spend time away from these gadgets? What do you find yourself turning to instead?

14. Become a volunteer for a local organization. Could you do this as a family?

15. Sort out the clothes in your closets and drawers. Can you give any to a charity?

16. Create your own designs for Easter card making. Help others to celebrate this time of year by sending them a card.

17. Cut up lots of thin strips of paper and ask each member of the family to write the name of a family member or friend on each separate piece. Put them in a box or jar and take one out each day to pray for that person.

18. Invite someone to your next Messy Church.

19. Think of God's creation and recycle more. Simplify your life.

20. Watch "One Solitary Life," a poem by James A. Francis, on YouTube (approximately three minutes).

21. Messy memorize: learn the Lord's Prayer together.

22. Which household chore do you dislike the most? Think of ways to make it more fun.

23. If you have a car, how could it be of use for someone who does not have one?

24. Messy media: think about your daily choices. Which TV programs do you watch? Which books do you read? Which websites do you regularly view? Are they a help to your spiritual growth?

25. Sort out your linen closet. Give old towels and blankets to animal charities.

26. Make a paper palm leaf, ready for Palm Sunday. Draw around your hand on green paper, cut out three hand shapes, and tape them (slightly overlapping) to a green drinking straw. (There are also many palm leaf templates on the Internet.)

27. Visit someone who is housebound.

28. Join some exercise classes and check out your personal health.

29. Begin to create an Easter garden for Easter Sunday. You will need a clay/plastic/foil saucer, a small clay/plastic pot, soil, pebbles, grass seed, six small sticks, string, and a stone. Place the soil in a mound on the saucer and tuck the pot into the soil to make a cave. Place the stone across the pot opening. Spread pebbles around the front and sides of the mound. Add seed to the soil and spray regularly with water. Tie the sticks together with string to make three small crosses and push them into the back of the mound of soil. Regularly sprayed with water, the grass takes seven to ten days to sprout.

30. Sort out the toys in your home to donate to local organizations.

31. Supermarket checkout: include an extra item in your cart each time you shop to donate to your local foodbank.

32. On Palm Sunday, talk about all the times your family have enjoyed celebrations. How did you celebrate? Write down those celebrations on the back of your palm leaf. How did you show your excitement? Read Matthew 21:1–11. How did the crowds show their excitement as Jesus entered Jerusalem?

33. At the Last Supper, Jesus shared food with his friends. Design a placemat for a friend, using cardstock or paper. After coloring it, laminate it to make it wipe-clean. Perhaps draw a caterpillar on one side and a butterfly on the other: turn over to show the butterfly on Easter Sunday.

34. Bake bread together using bread mix on Maundy Thursday, when Jesus broke bread with his friends.

35. Watch www.friendsandheroes.com/us/easter-video (three minutes).

36. Share a copy of Leonardo da Vinci's *Last Supper* painting and learn the names of all of the disciples.

37. Eat hot cross buns together to remember Jesus dying on the cross.

38. Decorate a plain white tablecloth or sheet, ready for the family meal on Easter Sunday.

39. Happy Easter! Roll away the stone on your grassy Easter garden. Use candles on Easter cakes, remembering that the disciples thought the light of Jesus had died forever on Good Friday—but on Easter his light shone again and is still shining now.

40. Search the Internet for lots more family Lent and Easter activities.

Shrovetide

Mardi Gras is French for "Fat Tuesday." It is celebrated in many countries as a time of carnival and feasting before Lent begins. The Mardi Gras season begins at Epiphany and ends the Tuesday before Ash Wednesday.

In the United Kingdom, the three days preceding Ash Wednesday are known as Shrovetide. Tuesday is known as Shrove Tuesday and is often called Pancake Day.

During Lent there were many foods that Christians traditionally would not eat—fish, meat, eggs, fats, and milk—and people would use up these foods on Shrove Tuesday so that no food was wasted. Pancakes were particularly associated with Shrove Tuesday as they used up eggs, fats, and milk. Pancake Day has been practiced for more than five hundred years.

If your Messy Church falls close to or on Shrove Tuesday, or if you want to include activities about Pancake Day or Mardi Gras in a Lent theme, here are some suggestions.

Tin can pancakes

You will need:

Tin cans, tea lights, matches, tools, oil, pancake mix, knives, oven gloves, pancake toppings such as sugar, syrup, or fruit.

How to

Remove the lid from one end of a tin can and empty contents. Wash and dry the tin. Make four to six holes in the sides of the tin near the top, using a traditional can opener to make an initial hole and a screwdriver-type tool to make the hole larger. Repeat near the bottom of the tin. Light a tea light and place the tin over it. Beware! The tin will become very hot. Use oven gloves.

Place a small amount of cooking oil in the center of the top of the upturned tin. Test to see if it is hot by dripping on a tiny amount of ready-prepared pancake mixture. If it sizzles, place one teaspoon of pancake mixture on the tin. Do not be tempted to add more mixture than this as it will take too long to cook. Use a knife to loosen the pancake as it cooks and turn frequently until it is browned on both sides. Eat with chosen toppings.

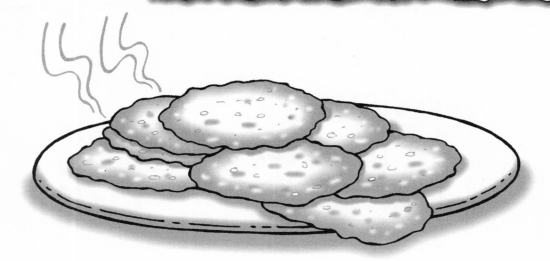

Toss 'n' time

You will need:

Frying pan, cardboard pancake circle or real pancake, and egg/kitchen timer.

How to

Set the timer for one minute and see how many times you can toss the pancake. The person who achieves the most tosses in the craft activities hour is the winner.

Flip the pancakes

You will need:

Pairs of cardboard pancake circles (see illustration) and spatula.

How to

Take half of the cardboard pancakes and draw, stick, or write a number or simple picture on each one. Then copy the numbers or pictures on the remaining pancakes to create matching pairs. Shuffle the cardboard pancakes and place them face down on the floor or large table. Take it in turns to flip two pancakes over each time, using the spatula, to find the matching pairs.

Mardi Gras masks

Enjoy the carnival theme with flamboyant masks embossed with glitter and feathers. There are many mask templates on the Internet, both full-face and partial.

Mardi Gras decorations

Decorate your space with paper chains, wreaths, baubles, stars, beads, napkins, plates, flowers, and streamers. The main Mardi Gras colors are purple (justice), green (faith), and gold (power). Look out for decorations in these colors in the post-Christmas sales.

Mardi Gras shakers

Make lots of noise with paper cup, plastic bottle, or paper plate shakers. (To make paper plate shakers, fold a plate in half, put half a cup of dried rice inside, and secure the edges with tape.) Decorate with Mardi Gras colored streamers.

Mardi Gras hats

Make hats in the favorite Mardi Gras styles—jester hats or crowns. Crowns represent the three kings at Epiphany; the colors of the jewels should be purple and green on gold.

Mardi Gras king cake

King cake is traditionally eaten in France, Spain, and the United States during the seasons of Epiphany and Mardi Gras. King cake parties are popular. The cake is a cinnamon roll covered in purple, green, and gold icing and sprinkles. Inside there is a hidden trinket, usually a small plastic baby to represent the Christ-child.

For Messy Church, alternatives could be king cupcakes, cinnamon doughnuts, or muffins with purple, green, and gold sprinkles.

Holy Week Messy Church

- **Theme:** Focusing on the last days of Lent and how Jesus surprises us in all that he does.

- **Biblical story:** Jesus arrives in Jerusalem, has supper with his friends, and is arrested and crucified.

- **Equipping today's families:** Jesus surprises us by his ability to love us for who we are, despite our failures, weaknesses, fears, and failures.

The Bible passages for these stories are:

- Matthew 21:1–11 (the triumphal entry)
- Matthew 26:14–16; John 13:27–30 (Judas agrees to betray Jesus)
- Luke 22:7–23 (the Last Supper)
- Matthew 26:36–68; 27:11–66; John 18:1–14; 18:28—19:42 (Gethsemane, arrest, trial, crucifixion, death, and burial)

Crafts

Gateway to Jerusalem

You will need:

Lots of empty cardboard boxes

How to

Help each other to build a large gateway to Jerusalem.

Talk about how Jesus entered Jerusalem on a donkey, possibly through the East Gate, also known as the Golden Gate or Beautiful Gate. There were nine gateways into Jerusalem, but the East Gate was sealed in 1541 and is still closed. It is believed that when Jesus returns he will enter Jerusalem once more through this gate. Jesus surprised everyone by riding on a humble donkey, a symbol of peace, instead of a horse, a symbol of war.

Fruity palm trees

You will need:

Paper plates, bananas, kiwi fruit, green apples, and rice cereals.

How to

Create a palm tree on the paper plate: first slice a peeled banana in half lengthways, then place half on the plate for the trunk. Slice the trunk into chunks to create a palm bark effect. Then make branches from segmented kiwi fruit or apples. Sprinkle rice cereal at the base to look like sand.

Talk about how the people cut down palm branches and laid them across Jesus' path or waved them in the air as he entered Jerusalem. They greeted him as a king and thought he would save them from the Romans. Palm branches signified goodness and victory and were often depicted on coins and important buildings. But Jesus was not there to kick out the Romans—he had come to die. This would have surprised the Palm Sunday crowds. They wanted Jesus to come and make them happy, but Jesus came to make us holy and whole.

Hosanna banners

You will need:

Large sheets of white material, markers, stickers, and cardstock templates of the letters H, o, s, a, and n.

How to

Lay the sheet of material flat on a table, draw around the templates to form the word "Hosanna" on the banner, and decorate.

Talk about how the people who welcomed Jesus on Palm Sunday shouted "Hosanna," which means "Save us!" They thought Jesus would save them from the Romans. Jesus would surprise them later, though, as he had come not as a political leader but as a spiritual one.

Judas coins

You will need:

Large sheet of paper, crayons, and coins.

How to

Invite everyone to draw around a coin and alongside the coin shape write something people do that disappoints us. See if you can cover the paper with thirty disappointments, representing each of the coins given to Judas for betraying Jesus.

Talk about how Judas betrayed Jesus on the night of the Last Supper. He told the high priests that he would give Jesus to them and was paid thirty pieces of silver. Jesus knew that this would happen and even told the disciples so as they sat and ate with him. Jesus still loved Judas, though, and wants us to forgive those who hurt us.

Betrayal cookies

You will need:

Paper plates, plain cookies, ready-made icing, candy, and sprinkles.

How to

Break a cookie in half and attempt to join it together again by binding it with icing. If you manage to do this, celebrate by decorating the whole cookie.

Talk about how when a friendship is broken, Jesus wants us to mend it and forgive. How easy or hard is this? At the Last Supper with his disciples, Jesus said, "A new command I give you: Love one another. As I have loved you, so you must love one another" (John 13:34).

Teardrop prayers

You will need:

Piles of heavy books, teardrop paper shapes, and pencils.

How to

Lift a pile of books to feel how heavy they are (with appropriate care for health and safety). Imagine them being so heavy that you couldn't lift them at all. Jesus felt the weight of sadness on him. He was going to die. Write a prayer to Jesus on the teardrop shape. You will need your prayer for the celebration time later.

Talk about how we can pray to God when we are troubled. Jesus was very sad about what was going to happen to him and he prayed to God, which gave him the courage to carry on. Jesus prayed in a garden where he knew he would be arrested. He surprises us by not giving up, even though many people turn their backs on him.

Disciple dip

You will need:

Shallow bowls, full-fat milk, assortment of food colorings (yellow, green, blue, red), dish soap, and cotton swabs.

How to

Pour enough full-fat milk to cover the bottom of a shallow bowl. Allow the milk to settle. Add various drops of food coloring near the center of the milk. Dip a cotton swab into some dish soap and put it in the food coloring. Watch the colors radiate away from the stick. Do not stir the mixture.

Talk about how Jesus' friends turned their backs on him after their last supper together. Judas left to tell the high priests where to find Jesus; the disciples fell asleep instead of keeping watch while Jesus prayed, and ran off when he was arrested; and Pontius Pilate washed his hands of Jesus when he had a near-riot on his hands, sending Jesus to his death. But Jesus did not give up on us.

Domino run

You will need:

Numerous boxes of dominoes or empty breakfast cereal boxes.

How to

If you only have enough space for tables, stand each domino on its end in a line across the tables, close together so that when you push over one it hits the next, causing the whole line to fall over. Create your own run designs. If you have floor space, set up the cereal boxes about eight inches apart and push one over to create a chain reaction.

Talk about how Jesus endured a chain of events that ended with his death on the cross. As you set up each domino run, recall all that Jesus had to go through during Holy Week. When did Jesus surprise you most?

Heart of nails

You will need:

Pieces of soft wood, round bright or roofers' nails (flat-topped), cardboard heart templates; colored string, embroidery thread, or wool; and selection of different-sized hammers.

How to

Choose a piece of wood and lay a heart template on top. Choose a number of nails and hammer them into the wood, outlining the heart shape as symmetrically as possible. Hammer the nails into the wood deep enough to stand proud but firm (supervise children). Remove the heart template. Weave the thread around the heads of the nails to outline a border, then from one side of the heart to another, creating your own design. If you wish to make a 3D design, push the thread to the bottom of the nail and then repeat weaving at the top of the nail.

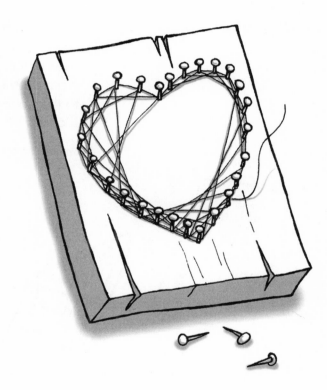

Talk about how Good Friday turns bad into good. Jesus dying on the cross for us was the best worst thing ever. Jesus never did anything wrong, but he loves us so much that he suffered the nails of the cross in his flesh because of all the wrong things we do.

Read all about it!

You will need:

Sheets of newspapers and markers.

How to

Place a sheet of newspaper in front of you with the short end at the top. Fold one top corner right over to the opposite side to make a point at the top. Crease well. Fold the top point over to the opposite side to make a roof shape. Crease well. From halfway down each side of the roof, tear straight down to the bottom of the page. Unfold the newspaper to discover a cross. Write "Jesus is alive" on the newspaper cross.

Talk about how we all need to share the good news of Jesus. His next surprise is that he will come back to life on Easter! The newspaper is full of news, but the good news of Jesus is the best news of all.

Celebration

Get ready

As people enter the celebration space, play a slide show of pictures of the crafts and activities that everyone has been doing. Explain that a lot of things happened to Jesus during Holy Week. We have seen Jesus enter Jerusalem, discovered how it feels to be betrayed, and learned about how Jesus died on the cross.

Go

You will need:

A storyteller and actors to play Jesus, eleven disciples, Judas, and five men with swords.

Invite volunteers to act out the events of the night of Maundy Thursday in the garden of Gethsemane. Then tell the story with your actors as follows.

Welcome to the garden of Gethsemane. Over here (point behind yourself) we have the Mount of Olives. Over here (point to one side) we have old Jerusalem. All around us are olive trees. Jesus came to this garden whenever he wanted to find a peaceful place to pray to God. Jesus talked to God his Father a lot, but on this night after his last meal with his friends the disciples, Jesus prayed so hard that he sweated blood. He knew how he was going to die.

Here are Jesus and his disciples. They have been in a room celebrating the annual Passover feast, their last supper together. Jesus asked them to eat bread and remember his body, and to drink wine and remember his blood.

The disciples are sad because Jesus has told them he is going to die. They can't quite believe it. They have sung together, then they have come here into the garden.

But look, one of the disciples is missing! Which one can it be?

Jesus asks the disciples to pray and watch over him as he prays to God. He takes Peter, James, and John farther into the garden, asking them to pray and keep watch. Jesus prays hard, as he is stressed and troubled. He knows how and when he is going to die.

When Jesus returns to the disciples, they have fallen asleep. Jesus says, "Could you not keep watch for one hour?"

Again he goes away to pray, and again he comes back to find them asleep because they are so tired. They do not know what to say to him.

After the third time he has gone to pray and come back again, Jesus wakes them, telling them that his betrayer is on the way.

Here comes Judas! He has brought men with swords. He kisses and greets Jesus to show them who Jesus is. The men seize Jesus and arrest him. Jesus tells them that it is happening as planned—he knows how he is going to die—but the disciples run away.

The next day, Jesus will be crucified on a cross.

Holy Week has been full of surprises for the people in Jerusalem, the disciples, and for us, but Jesus always knew how things were going to happen. And on Easter Jesus gives us the best surprise of all: he is alive!

Prayer of tears

It is time to find the prayer that you wrote on a teardrop shape earlier. Sandwich it between your praying hands. Press your hands together so tightly that it hurts—harder and harder. Jesus prayed to God so hard that he sweated blood. Release your hands and look at your prayer. Now a leader will pray:

Dear Jesus, we don't want to turn our backs on you. We don't want to let you down. We know that you suffered so much for us. Thank you for having the courage to do God's will. Forgive us for all the things we do wrong, and help us to be more like you. Amen.

Finish with the Messy Grace:

May the grace of our Lord Jesus Christ *(hold out your hands as if expecting a gift)*
And the love of God *(put your hands on your heart)*
And the fellowship of the Holy Spirit *(hold hands)*
Be with us all now and for ever. Amen! *(raise hands together on the word "Amen")*

Cards to put on the meal table

- What did you like best about Messy Church today?
- Jesus' friends fell asleep three times when he had asked them to pray and watch over him. How do you think they felt when Judas came with men and swords to arrest Jesus?
- Where do you think the disciples went when Jesus was crucified? The Bible only tells us about John being present.
- We can pray to God anytime and anywhere. Where is your favorite praying place?
- Jesus surprises us on Easter! How does that make you feel?

Take-home ideas

Lenten cross challenge

You will need:

Eleven plastic cups (plus a few extra), purple construction paper, and table tennis balls.

How to

Stand up the eleven cups to create a cross shape. Fold a roll of purple paper inside each cup to form a purple Lenten cross. Place extra cups around the cross. Stand at a distance and try to bounce table tennis balls into the purple cups.

Talk about the color purple and how Jesus was given a purple robe to wear when the soldiers mocked him. They did not understand that he was the Son of God.

Other ideas

- **Endurance test:** Jesus' endurance on Good Friday was incredible. Find a family activity that you could challenge each other to complete (for example, board games, cycling, or chess tournament).

- **Passover meal:** Discover what happens at a Passover meal and enjoy the exodus Bible story together (Exodus 13–14).

- **Jesus died for me:** On Good Friday morning, find a red marker and mark a spot in the middle of your palm. Write your name across the red spot in another color. Remember how Jesus died for each of us.

- **Crown of thorns cookies:** Create a crown to remember how Jesus suffered on Good Friday. Spread a round sugary cookie with peanut butter (be aware of allergies) or chocolate spread. Break pretzels into pieces and arrange them like thorns around the edge of the cookie.

- **Holy cross:** The cross is the strongest and most powerful Christian symbol. Use circle-shaped cereal pieces to cover a cross template. Remember how holy Jesus wants us to be.

- **Hot cross buns:** Whether you bake them or buy them, enjoy eating hot cross buns together. The baking process, with several waiting periods in which the dough has to rise, reminds us that each of the separate events Jesus had to experience in Holy Week was significant on his journey to the cross.

Easter Messy Church

- **Theme:** The excitement of Jesus being alive!

- **Biblical story:** The resurrection and the witnesses on Easter.

- **Equipping today's families:** Encouraging people to think about the spiritual as well as the material side of Easter and to see Jesus in their everyday lives. Jesus is at the heart of Easter and is ultimately all that matters.

The Bible passages for these stories are Matthew 28:1–15; Mark 16:1–18; Luke 24:1–49; and John 20:1–31.

Crafts

Salt painting

You will need:

Table salt, white glue, watercolor paints, food colorings, paintbrushes, jars of clean water, and construction paper.

How to

Dribble lines of glue around the paper to create a picture. Next, sprinkle table salt over the glue. Shake away any excess salt. Using a brush dipped in watercolors, touch the salt lines and watch the salt soak up the colors. Do not drag the brush through the glue and salt, but just touch lightly. Change colors or experiment with food coloring mixed with a little water.

Talk about how the salty tears of the disciples and family of Jesus on Good Friday are changed to joy and wonder on Easter Sunday as the tomb is found empty and Jesus lives.

Rolling the stone

You will need:

Paint, marbles or golf balls, paper, foil trays, long cardboard tubes, and masking tape.

How to

Dip the marbles or balls in paint and roll or shake them on the paper to make abstract pictures. This activity can be arranged on a grand scale with rolls of paper spread along the floor. Use cardboard tubes and masking tape to make buffers around the edges. For individuals, it is fun to put paint into a foil tray or pan and shake the marbles in it.

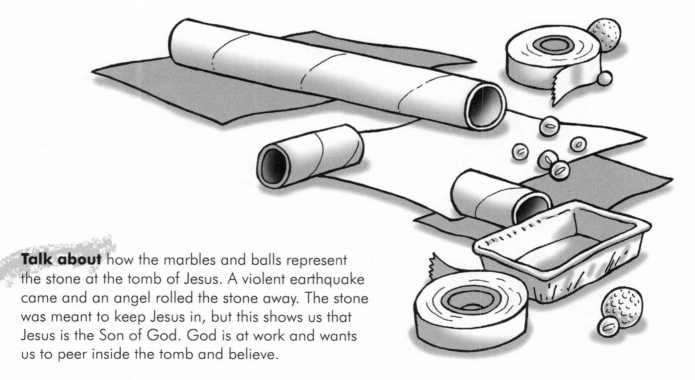

Talk about how the marbles and balls represent the stone at the tomb of Jesus. A violent earthquake came and an angel rolled the stone away. The stone was meant to keep Jesus in, but this shows us that Jesus is the Son of God. God is at work and wants us to peer inside the tomb and believe.

Cross suncatcher prayer

You will need:

Laminating machine (to be operated with the assistance of an adult team member), laminator pouches, colored cellophanes or candy wrappings, printouts of John 8:12, sequins, tissue paper, flower petals, paper, pencils, permanent marker, hole punch, strong scissors, and ribbon.

How to

Switch on the laminating machine. Lay patterns of decorative materials in the pouch. It may be helpful to draw a cross shape on the pouch with the permanent marker, as a guide. Add a printout of John 8:12. On another small piece of paper, write a prayer about Jesus on the cross, and add this to the pattern. Put the pouch through the laminator. From the pouch, cut out a large cross shape or a few smaller crosses. Make a hole in the top, tie ribbon through, and hang near a window.

I am the light for the world! Follow me, and you won't be walking in the dark.

Talk about the awe and wonder of Easter, and the joy and jubilation felt by Mary Magdalene when Jesus appeared to her at the tomb.

Easter memory game

You will need:

A tray, a pile of three silver coins, a bar of soap, a large nail, olives, a bread roll, a dice, a small wooden cross, a round rock, a piece of purple cloth, an angel figure, and a covering cloth.

How to

Place all ten items on the tray and cover with a cloth. Invite a group of all ages to sit around your table/space. Uncover the tray and ask everyone to memorize the items. Cover the tray once more. Pick up the tray and turn it around, carefully removing one item and hiding it so that no one can see. Turn back and remove the cover from the tray. Ask, what is missing? When someone answers correctly, produce the missing item and talk about its significance in the Easter story. Repeat with all items.

Talk about the meaning of the Easter items on the tray.

- Silver coins: Judas, a disciple of Jesus, betrayed him to the religious leaders for thirty pieces of silver.
- Soap: Jesus surprised the disciples and washed their feet before their last supper together. Also, Pontius Pilate washed his hands as a symbol to say that he was not responsible for sending Jesus to his death.
- Bread: On Maundy Thursday, Jesus shared bread and wine with his disciples and said, "Take and eat; this represents my body." Churches offer bread and wine in a service of Holy Communion, where we can remember what Jesus did for us.
- Olives: Jesus went to the Mount of Olives to pray. He knew that Judas and the soldiers would find him there and arrest him.
- Purple cloth: Jesus was taken from courtroom to courtroom early on Good Friday. He was dressed in a purple robe and a crown made of thorns by the soldiers. They mocked him for looking like a king. Jesus had not denied that he was king of the Jews.
- Dice: When Jesus was on the cross, the soldiers played a game to win Jesus' clothes. They did this in front of him. How did they feel about Jesus?
- Cross: Jesus died on a cross, and we use the symbol of the cross as a reminder of what he did for us.
- Nail: Nails held Jesus on the cross. A nail also held the sign "Jesus of Nazareth, King of the Jews" on the cross.
- Rock: When Jesus was buried, he had a stone covering his tomb entrance—but no stone can stop Jesus, the Son of God.
- Angel: When Easter came, an angel told Mary and Mary Magdalene that Jesus had risen.

Which other items from the Easter story could be placed on the tray?

Empty tomb treats

You will need:

Mini doughnuts, chocolate spread, small round cookies, crackers, shredded coconut, green food coloring, and plastic food bags.

Talk about how Joseph of Arimathea donated his own burial place to Jesus after the crucifixion. Joseph received permission from Pontius Pilate to take Jesus' body from the cross. He wrapped Jesus in fine linen and applied myrrh and aloes before placing him in a burial tomb (a cave) and sealing the entrance with a stone. Doing the right thing for God was risky for Joseph.

How to

Create a tomb by spreading chocolate spread on a cracker, slicing a piece from a doughnut to stand up on the cracker, placing a cookie to one side of the tomb entrance, and sprinkling grass around the tomb. To make the grass, place shredded coconut in a food bag, add green food coloring, and shake until the coconut turns green.

Messy cream eggs

You will need:

A tray, shaving cream, window squeegee, paints, egg-shaped cardstock, plastic forks, towels, and cloths.

How to

Squirt shaving cream on to the base of the tray and spread it smoothly. Add squirts of paint on top of the cream. Use a fork to stir the colors around. Place the egg-shaped cardstock on top of the mixture. Press down to make sure the cream mixture has contact with the entire cardstock. Lift the cardstock off and wait approximately one minute. Use the squeegee to slowly and carefully scrape off the shaving cream. Wash or wipe the squeegee in between each scrape. The egg will look as if it is marbled.

Talk about how in medieval times, eggs were a forbidden food during Lent. This meant that they were often included in Easter meals. Chocolate Easter eggs are now a popular Easter gift. Eggs also symbolize new life, and Jesus brings new life to each of us if we believe in him.

Clay crosses

You will need:

Air-hardening clay, clay-cutting tools or blunt knives, sequins, small beads, and paper plates.

How to

Roll out a small piece of clay and form a cross shape with a cutting tool or knife. Press small beads and sequins into the clay until the surface is encrusted. Take home the cross on a paper plate to dry.

Talk about how the cross made of plain clay reminds us of the pain and suffering of Jesus as he died on a wooden cross. But as you decorate your cross with bright beads and sequins, you transform death into life, as Jesus transformed us at Easter time.

Butterflies

You will need:

Butterfly template (page 90), wrapping paper (not the foil kind), yarn, and scissors.

How to

The template may not look like a butterfly yet, but it will become one. Place the template on some wrapping paper, draw around it, and cut out the shape. Starting at the narrow end, accordian-fold the shape, creasing each fold well and keeping them narrow. Fold the completed shape in half and tie the center with some yarn. Gently open the butterfly wings and pinch the center at each side to keep the butterfly in shape.

Talk about how Jesus surprised Mary and Mary Magdalene on Easter morning when the tomb was empty. As the strange shape of the template is transformed into a beautiful butterfly, so Jesus transformed the lives of people on earth. His life began when he was a small baby, symbolized by a caterpillar; he was crucified and died, symbolized by a cocoon; and he rose again as a butterfly rises into the sky, drying its new wings.

Earth-shaking changes

You will need:

Empty clean jars with tight lids, cup, heavy cream, spoon, bowls, food bags, and salt (optional).

Talk about how, on Easter morning, there was a violent earthquake and an angel of the Lord rolled back the tombstone to show that the tomb was empty. The guards were afraid and also shook. As you watch the changing stages in the butter-making, think about the perseverance of Jesus on the cross, knowing that he was going to die but would change the world by showing us his love.

How to

Pour a quarter of a cup of heavy cream into the jar. Screw the lid on tightly and shake the jar vigorously. Keep shaking until the cream looks thick and coats the sides of the jar. This is whipped cream. (Since this stage may take a while, you may wish to pre-prepare some jars to this point, or simply have one or two that you hand from person to person rather than giving everyone their own.) Continue shaking until the cream resembles cottage cheese. Keep shaking until you hear a splash: the cream has lumped together and there is also a puddle of milk. This stage can happen in just a few seconds. Continue shaking until you are confident that the cream has separated into butter and milk.

Pour off the milk and place the butter into a bowl. Press a spoon on to the butter to squeeze out any excess milk. Salt to taste and stir it well. Take home in a sealed food bag and spread on warm bread or toast.

Doubting pictures

You will need:

Printouts of some optical illusion pictures (see below; there are plenty of others on the Internet).

How to

Invite all ages to look at the pictures. Can you really be sure what you are looking at?

Talk about how Thomas was missing when Jesus revealed himself to the disciples in Galilee. Thomas did not believe them when they told him Jesus was alive. When Jesus came to them all again, he asked Thomas to touch his wounds to prove that he was the Son of God. Talk about how Jesus would have looked after he came back to life on Easter morning. Would he still have had his earthly body? Did everyone recognize him?

Celebration

Get ready

As people enter the celebration space, play a slide show of pictures of the crafts and activities that everyone has been doing. Play joyful music. Give everyone a small printout of an optical illusion picture of Jesus (you can find these on the Internet) and explain that it will be needed for the prayer time. Explain how the crafts were chosen to help us to think about the joy and excitement felt by Mary (mother of Jesus), Mary Magdalene, and the disciples when Jesus rose from the dead. They saw Jesus—but who sees Jesus now?

Go

Invite volunteers to be Richie (or Rachel) the reporter (with a roving microphone or one made from a cardboard tube with a tennis ball taped to one end), Mary the mother of Jesus (Mary 1), Mary Magdalene (Mary 2), Thomas, and Messy Messenger (wearing running shoes and carrying a mobile phone). Hand out copies of the following script.

Richie (or Rachel):	So here we are in AD 33 in Galilee. My name is Richie [or Rachel] the reporter. Sadly, TV has not been invented yet, or the newspaper printer, so instead we have our Messy Messenger, the fastest runner in Galilee! *(Messy Messenger runs fast on the spot, showing off.)* Oh yes, just look at those fast running shoes! He/she will be able to run and tell this exciting story to the whole country in . . . well . . . how long do you reckon?
Messenger:	A couple of days.
Richie:	*(Looking shocked.)* A couple of days? It will be old news by then!
Messenger:	Well, how much are you paying me?
Richie:	Thirty pieces of silver—shekels to you.
Messenger:	Why does that amount sound familiar? *(Pause.)* Okay, a couple of hours, then.
Richie:	Much better. Now listen up . . . what are you doing now?

Messenger:	*(Pointing a mobile phone at everyone like a camera.)* It came free with my new running shoes. I can record you all. Speak up, everyone!
Richie:	Well, I feel that today is going to be full of surprises! So let's say hello to Thomas, Mary . . . and Mary! Seems to be a popular name. Any reason why?
Mary 1:	Lots of girls are named Mary; they have been for years! There are nine Marys mentioned in the Bible.
Richie:	I see. *(Pause.)* Okay, so tell us who you are, why we are here, and why you are all looking so happy.
Mary 1:	I'm Mary, mother of Jesus. I saw my son die on the cross on Friday, and today he is alive!
Richie:	That's amazing! No wonder you're smiling! But how can this be?
Mary 1:	Because he is the Son of God.
Mary 2/Thomas:	Yes, yes, it's true!
Richie:	Right, right, so let's ask you, Mary number two! Who are you?
Mary 2:	I'm Mary Magdalene, friend and follower of Jesus. I also saw Jesus die on the cross on Friday, and indeed he is alive again.
Mary 1/Thomas:	Alive! Alive!
Richie:	Mmm, I'm sensing great excitement here. This Jesus, Son of God, definitely died but now he is alive again. I hope you're getting all of this, Messy Messenger? So, how do you know he is alive?
Mary 1:	We saw him. We touched him.
Mary 2:	The burial tomb was empty, and then he came to us.
Thomas:	They saw him before I did. I'm a bit embarrassed, really.
Richie:	There, there, don't be embarrassed, Thomas. Are you getting this, Messy Messenger? So, Thomas, tell us who you are and what happened.
Thomas:	I'm Thomas, one of Jesus' disciples. I've been following Jesus and learning from him for three years now, but I didn't believe the other disciples when they told me Jesus was alive.
Richie:	So Jesus showed himself to the disciples too? Where were you?
Thomas:	It doesn't matter where I was. But I missed him and wouldn't believe it until I saw him for myself. I was so embarrassed. Jesus knew I hadn't believed it. He asked me to touch his wounds to prove he was alive—in front of all the other disciples. He told us that he was going to be with us all forevermore.

Mary 1/Mary 2:	Forever!
Messenger:	*(Running fast on the spot.)* Right then. I'm off to tell this story. Can't wait! It's very exciting.
Thomas:	But wait, there's more.
Mary 1:	Yes, so much more.
Mary 2:	Jesus appeared to lots more people, and there was a miraculous catching of fish. And we haven't told you about the earthquake and the angel yet.
Messenger:	But my phone batteries are dying and this is the only evidence I have of this story being true.
Thomas:	But we've just told you. Isn't that enough? Don't be like me. I didn't believe— but it is true. Jesus is alive and he is the Son of God.
Richie:	Go on, Messy Messenger. We can always arrange another interview time. Go and share the good news. Be quick! Get running! You may see Jesus too.

Illusion prayer

Ask everyone to look at the optical illusion picture of Jesus that was given to them earlier (you may prefer to use a slide show version instead). You may need to tell people to focus on the middle of the picture for a few seconds, then look to a bright wall and blink a few times. What can you see?

Dear Jesus, we have heard the story of your death. We were sad. We have heard the story of how you came alive again. We were overjoyed. We have heard that you will be with us forever. We were excited. Help us not to be like Thomas, who doubted, but to be more like Mary and Mary and see you in our lives each day. Thank you for Easter morning! Amen.

Sing a song to remember how Jesus asked Thomas to touch his wounds to help him to believe. The Bible doesn't tell us if Thomas actually did this. What do you think?

Finish with the Messy Grace:

May the grace of our Lord Jesus Christ *(hold out your hands as if expecting a gift)*
And the love of God *(put your hands on your heart)*
And the fellowship of the Holy Spirit *(hold hands)*
Be with us all now and for ever. Amen! *(raise hands together on the word "Amen")*

Cards to put on the meal table

- What did you like best about Messy Church today?
- Which part of the Easter story made you feel excited?
- Which part of the Easter story surprised you?
- How do you think Thomas felt when he knew that the other disciples had seen Jesus before he had?
- Where might you see Jesus now?

Take-home ideas

Angel bottle

You will need:

Empty water bottles, paper plates, doilies, clear tape, silver glitter, silver chenille stick, and silver ribbon.

How to

Remove the water bottle label and fill the bottle three quarters full with water. Add glitter and screw the top on tight. Create angel wings using a paper plate and/or doily and stick them on the back of the bottle using clear tape. Make a halo shape with the chenille stick and wrap it around the bottle neck. Decorate with silver ribbons. Shake the bottle and see the glitter move and settle.

Talk about how on Easter morning, there was a violent earthquake and an angel of the Lord came down from heaven. The burial tomb was empty. Jesus appeared to his mother Mary and Mary Magdalene. Shake the angel bottle to remind yourself of this awesome experience. Read in the Bible about the many times Jesus appeared to people after he rose from the dead. Each time, shake the angel bottle and imagine the awe and wonder that they experienced.

Earthquake detector

You will need:

Large adhesive googly eyes, cardstock, markers, and removable adhesive tack.

Talk about how most of us don't know when we will experience an earthquake or other natural disaster. It was a surprise for those at Jesus' tomb to experience an earthquake and for an angel to tell them that Jesus had risen. Are we ready for the time when Jesus comes back to earth? How would we detect it if it happened?

How to

Cut out a piece of cardstock approximately four by four inches. Attach two googly eyes, and underneath write:

- The location of a first aid kit
- "In an emergency dial 911" (or appropriate emergency phone number)

Attach the card to a highly visible wall.

Egg drop

You will need:

Lots of eggs, assortment of protective wrappings (for example, bubble wrap, kitchen wrap, egg boxes, brown packing paper, computer paper, paper cloth wipes, coffee filter paper), and pencils.

How to

Experiment with ways to prevent an egg from breaking by wrapping it in different materials, dropping it, and recording your findings. This experiment is best done outdoors on protected ground (spread with plastic sheeting or unused garbage bags).

Talk about how Joseph of Arimathea risked a lot by asking Pontius Pilate for Jesus' body and wrapping it in linen to place in his tomb (John 19:38–42). Joseph was a member of the Supreme Court in ancient Israel and yet he followed Jesus. His faith in God outweighed his fear of the court and the Roman rulers.

Celebrate Easter together

Invite family and friends together to celebrate Easter with a party and festive food. Alternatively, arrange a family outing or think about how you could serve people in the community by offering voluntary time in some way.

Creative Easter Prayers

- **Sorry sand prayers:** Sprinkle a small amount of sand in trays and invite people to write "sorry" with their finger, or draw a sad face as they share with God things they have done wrong. Shake the tray and watch the pattern disappear. God forgives you as quickly as that.

- **Foil cross:** Use the foil wrapping from Easter eggs or kitchen aluminium foil pieces. As you pray about all that Jesus did for us by dying on the cross, form a cross with the foil by rolling, tearing, or scrunching.

- **Butterfly prayers:** Jesus rose from the dead, brought us new life, and changed the world. Make a butterfly and, using colored pencils, write on it your hopes for the world (see template on page 90 and instructions on page 63).

- **Light prayer:** Light some birthday candles and explain how Jesus is the light of the world. The devil tried to take Jesus into the darkness but Jesus rose again on Easter morning. Jesus said, "I am the light of the world. Whoever follows me will never walk in darkness, but will have the light of life" (John 8:12).

- **Revealing prayer:** Moments of quiet focus can bring out emotions for all ages. This prayer helps to confirm that Jesus is always there for us, even in the dark times of our lives. Draw lots of lit candles on white paper with a white crayon. Wash over the whole paper with watered-down paint. The candles are revealed one by one. God said, "Let light shine out of darkness" (2 Corinthians 4:6).

- **Singing circle prayers:** Sit everyone in a circle. Take a well-known preschool tune and start a prayer in which everyone takes turns to sing a word. They have to make up each line of the prayer. This is great fun and also focuses on pattern, rhythm, trust, and encouragement. If anyone falters, others can help.

5

Easter Extras

Here are some extra ideas to use, including some very traditional ones that may bring back memories for some of you.

- **Easter cards:** Use the Internet to discover how many ways you can print, cut, pop up, decorate, sew, knit, and paint Easter cards. Who would love to receive a card celebrating this important event? Everyone! Don't forget those "thank you" cards for the people who gave you Easter gifts.

- **Easter candle:** The Paschal candle, also known as the Easter candle, is a large white candle that is renewed every Easter and then used around the year at baptisms, funerals, and other special times. Make your own Easter candle by creating a cross design on the side of a white candle, using a dull pencil. Press into the soft wax to create a relief effect. Paint over the design with a brush dipped in paint. Wipe away the excess with a babywipe. You could also insert five cloves, at the four points of the cross plus the center, to represent the five wounds of Christ.

- **Easter bonnets:** Bonnets are traditionally worn at Easter church services. Fun designs can be made from sheets of newspaper. You need two people to create this masterpiece. Hold down three sheets of newspaper on the head, splayed out to cover as much of the head as possible. Press down and mold the shape of the top of the head by creasing the newspaper to form a bowl shape. Attach some masking tape around the crown of the head in a circle. Roll up the newspaper brim, starting and ending at the back. Add tissue paper flowers, feathers, and so on.

- **Hobby donkey:** This is a Palm Sunday craft made from left and right profiles of a cardboard donkey head, attached to a pole with double-sided tape. Add black curly lashes and mane. Alternatively, stuff a grey sock with pillow filling and attach to insulation foam tubes.

- **Angels:** There are many angel templates on the Internet. If you have a very large sand pit, pour some sand into the bottom and invite people to lie down in it and wave their arms up and down like snow angels.

- **City of Jerusalem graffiti wall:** For Palm Sunday, make a graffiti wall from a large sheet of paper with brick outlines. What would the people of Jerusalem say about this king?

- **Fig Bibles:** It is believed that Jesus wanted to eat figs on his journey to Jerusalem on Palm Sunday. These edible Bibles are fun to make. Using a sharp knife, slice off the edge of one of the long lengths of a fig cookie. With icing, design a border along the front of the cookie, mark a cross in the center, and draw lines across the uncut long edge to look like the spine of a book. Make a sugar paste strip as a small bookmark and push it into the fig filling in the cookie.

- **Easter collage:** This is an opportunity to create a floor activity that all ages will enjoy. Choose any aspect of the Easter story and offer piles of materials such as paper, fabric, paints, pens, glue, and glitter that can be used to make a large collage. Ask your church congregation to save up collage materials so they can be used in more than one session.

- **Easter tree:** This is a tradition originating in Germany. Eggs symbolize new life. Place branches taken from bushes or trees into a vase or pot. Decorate with dyed eggs hanging from ribbons or plastic eggs containing treats. This is an ideal Lenten family activity in which eggs can be added each day.

- **Easter baskets:** Simple or complicated, there are lots of templates for folding baskets on the Internet. More simply, seal an envelope and cut off two corners to form a handle. Decorate and fill with chocolate eggs.

- **Water-resistant eggs:** Cut out egg shapes from white paper and draw a pattern on the paper with white crayons. Dip brushes into watercolor paint. Brush over the paper and watch the pattern appear.

- **Egg dyeing:** Draw a pattern on a hard-boiled egg with wax crayons or wrap rubber bands around the egg. Place the egg in a mixture of half a cup of boiling water, one teaspoon of white vinegar, and approximately twenty drops of food coloring. Leave the egg in the solution for around ten minutes for a paler color and thirty minutes for a stronger color. Use tongs to take the egg out of the solution and dry it on a wire rack. Eggs were traditionally not eaten during Lent, so any eggs that were not used up at Shrovetide were dyed and decorated and saved until Easter.

- **Bubblewrap eggs:** Cut out egg shapes from bubblewrap. Paint the bubble wrap and press a piece of paper on to the paint to make an egg print.

- **Free-range painting:** This is a popular Messy Church all-age activity. Roll paper up the wall and secure it with masking tape. Create enough paper space for three or four painters at a time. Offer plastic disposable aprons for the adults and children, as well as a selection of paints and brushes. Allow everyone to paint freely along with the theme. You will find that the very young children are drawn to this art form.

- **Cross crafts:** Crosses can be made from many different materials—for example, real nails bound together, craft sticks, wooden branches, mosaic pieces, beads, cross-stitch, stained glass, fun foam, chenille sticks with threaded beads, and scratch art.

6

Easter Food and Food Crafts

Edible Easter garden

You will need:

Paper plates, jelly beans, chocolate sticks, round cookie, marshmallow, green icing, and green napkins.

How to

Place a green napkin on the plate and crumple up another napkin to create a grassy hill. In front of the hill, secure the round cookie with green icing to seal the tomb. Make a cross by joining two chocolate sticks together with the icing and stand it in the marshmallow. Use the jelly beans to make a path for the characters in the Bible story.

Palm sundaes

You will need:

Green Jell-O to represent palm leaves, strawberry mousse, vanilla cookies to represent the dusty road, plastic food bags, plastic spoons, rolling pin, small jelly jars, whipped cream, and sprinkles.

How to

Put the vanilla cookies into a food bag and bash with a rolling pin to make crumbs. Layer all the ingredients together in jars, squirt cream on top, and add sprinkles.

Chocolate tombstone cake

You will need:

10 T salted butter
½ c cocoa powder
1¾ c sugar
1 c flour
3 eggs

How to

Preheat the oven to 350 degrees. Butter and flour an eight-inch round cake pan. In a pan on the stove, melt the butter. Add the rest of the ingredients and stir until combined. Pour the batter into the cake pan. Bake for twenty-five to thirty minutes. Eat as is or serve with ice cream.

Puff pastry eggs

You will need:

Ready-made shortcrust pastry, your favorite pie filling, egg, food coloring, thin artists' brushes, and oval cookie cutters.

How to

Heat the oven to 375 degrees. Roll out the pastry and cut out an even number of egg shapes. Place half the egg shapes on an ungreased baking sheet. Add one spoonful of pie filling to each egg shape, moisten the pastry edges with water, and place the remaining egg shapes on top. Seal the edges by pressing together. Separate the egg white from the yolk. Brush the egg white over the pastry tops and let dry. Mix food coloring with the egg yolk and paint Easter pictures on the top. Bake for ten to twelve minutes.

Other ideas

- **Easter egg nests:** Melt chocolate with rice cereal to create a nest in a paper muffin cup. Add small chocolate eggs.

- **Easter lollipops:** Dip lollipops into chocolate. Alternatively, push a lollipop stick into a large marshmallow and dip into lukewarm water. Shake off any surplus water and dip into sprinkles.

- **Easter cupcakes:** Decorate shop-bought cupcakes with butter icing and mini chocolate eggs.

- **Dipped pretzels:** Use tongs to dip pretzels into melted chocolate and place on wax paper. Add sprinkles and leave to dry. Place in the fridge for faster drying. They are yummy with white chocolate too.

Egg rolling

You will need:

A homemade sheet with a target drawn on it, hard-boiled eggs, and a prize.

How to

This game is eggs-tra thrilling because eggs do not roll in a straight line on a flat floor—they wiggle. Split your team into four small groups for heats. Each contestant rolls an egg along the floor (no throwing), aiming for the center of the target. The winner of each heat goes through to the final. The winner of the final gets the prize.

Egg hunt

You will need:

Lots of wrapped chocolate eggs or plastic eggs filled with treats, depending on the number of people expected; collecting bags, baskets, or containers.

How to

Think about which age groups you want to join in with the hunt. If the children are very young, the eggs need to be placed in obvious places—for example, on a grassy lawn. For older children, the eggs can be hidden, perhaps with additional clues. With adults, you could make the hiding places even harder, with additional cryptic clues or anagrams.

Tip: if you have all ages involved, state the ground rules clearly. It works well to use plastic eggs with certain colors for certain age groups. Some very young children are happier with assistance from older children and adults, especially if the hunt takes place over a large area such as in the woods.

Egg commands game

Explain the following six "egg" commands and actions.

- Scrambled: run around
- Fried: lie flat on your back
- Boiled: jump up and down
- Poached: curl up into a small ball
- Chocolate: rub tummy and pat head at the same time
- Omelette: all hold hands

To start the game, shout out each command. The last person to do the correct action, or anyone doing the wrong action, is out and becomes a game watcher to help the leader get everyone out.

Easter commands game

This has the same rules as the egg commands game, but the commands are as follows.

- Cross: stand with arms outstretched to the side
- Lent: run around six times to represent six weeks
- Joy: thumbs up
- Sadness: thumbs down
- Easter: curl up small like an egg
- Jesus is alive!: Hold someone's hands and spin around

Egg and spoon race

Split your teams into groups for heats. The first competitors start the relay from point A (one end of a room) and carry a hard-boiled egg in a spoon, with the other arm held behind the back, to point B.

At point B, the next person takes the spoon and carries the egg to point A. The winners of each heat go through to a final. To make the game more difficult, add obstacles.

Desert dash

Explain how the devil tempted Jesus in the desert with stones and by taking him high up on a roof and up a mountain, but Jesus turned to God and resisted the temptations. Place everyone in a circle, sitting down. Give everyone a word to remember, alternating "stones," "roof," and "mountain." Place a beanbag in the center of the circle. When one of the words is called out, the people who were given that word stand up and run around outside the circle, clockwise. When they reach the point where they were sitting, they enter the circle to grab the beanbag.

   This game also works well with a parachute: when you call out a word, those who were given that word run under the parachute as everyone else raises it high. When the people running under have grabbed the chute again, you call out another word. When you call out "God," everyone runs under at the same time and tries to grab the chute before it touches the floor.

Disciple ladders

You will need twenty-four people. Sit them down in pairs down the center of a room or area, allowing running space at either side. Ask them to face each other with arms folded, legs outstretched, and feet touching. Position each pair some distance away from the next to accommodate a stride or jump. Give each pair the name of a disciple and decide which end of the line is the top of the "ladder."

   Call out a disciple's name. Wherever that pair is on the "ladder," they stand and run up to the top of the "ladder," carefully striding or jumping over the pairs of legs; then each person runs down their own outside lane to the bottom of the "ladder" and back to their place. Be prepared to pause the game every time safety reminders are needed—to keep legs flat down on the floor and together.

Jerusalem gates

You need lots of space for this game. Explain how the city of Jerusalem has had its walls rebuilt many times and, at one time, had eleven gates. Play a game of tag in which one person is "it." If anyone is tagged, they "freeze" and become a gate with their feet apart. They cannot join in the game again unless someone crawls between their feet, the "gate." Continue the game until everyone is frozen. The last person to be frozen is "it" next.

Easter Trail

Many churches have created an Advent trail in which knitted sheep are placed in shops and family-friendly venues in the community. (See www.messychurch.org.uk for stories from Messy Churches who have shared their exciting experiences—there are some very creative ideas out there!) Adapt the idea for Lent and Holy Week with these suggestions. Involve your church community, local schools, uniformed organizations, and knitting groups.

- For an Easter trail, knit chickens or hens large enough to place in shops and windows. There are lots of free knitting patterns on the Internet.
- Include a printed sheet with the Easter story to take home.
- Give chocolate Easter eggs as prizes.
- Print dates of any Easter service, event, or Messy Church on the take-home sheet.
- During Lent or Holy Week, invite homes in the community to host an Easter storybook or movie each day. Knit lots of mini Easter angels and leave one at each home as the Easter story is passed on.

Craft Templates

Lenten cross

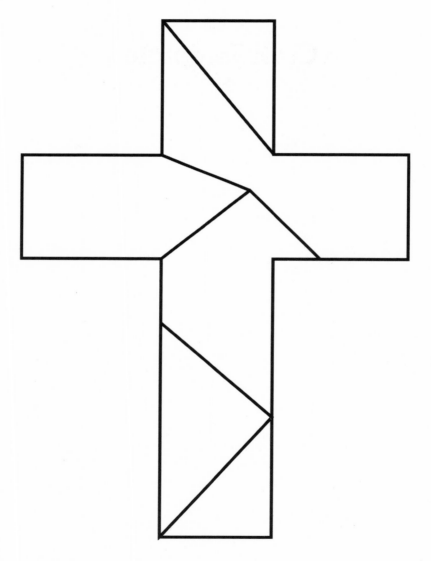

Remote control prayer

Reproduced with permission from *Messy Easter* by Jane Leadbetter (Messy Church, 2014).
Also available as a download from www.messychurch.org.uk/9781841017174/

Butterflies

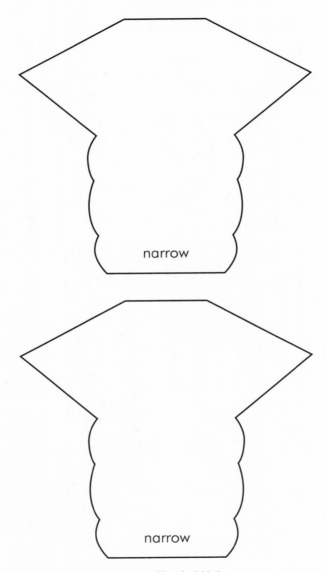

narrow

narrow

Index of Crafts and Games

ALSO AVAILABLE

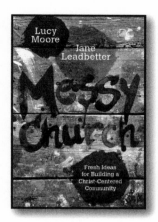

Messy Church
978-0-8308-4138-7

Messy Christmas
978-0-8308-4139-4

Doing church differently

BRF's Messy Church is a form of church that involves creativity, celebration, and hospitality, and enables people of all ages to belong to Christ together through their local church. It is particularly aimed at people who have never belonged to a church before.

Find out more at **messychurch.org.uk**.

IVP PRAXIS

EQUIPPING LEADERS FOR MINISTRY

"...TO EQUIP HIS PEOPLE FOR WORKS OF SERVICE,
SO THAT THE BODY OF CHRIST MAY BE BUILT UP."

EPHESIANS 4:12

God has called us to ministry. But it's not enough to have a vision for ministry if you don't have the practical skills for it. Nor is it enough to do the work of ministry if what you do is headed in the wrong direction. We need both vision *and* expertise for effective ministry. We need *praxis*.

Praxis puts theory into practice. It brings cutting-edge ministry expertise from visionary practitioners. You'll find sound biblical and theological foundations for ministry in the real world, with concrete examples for effective action and pastoral ministry. Praxis books are more than the "how to"—they're also the "why to." And because *being* is every bit as important as *doing*, Praxis attends to the inner life of the leader as well as the outer work of ministry. Feed your soul, and feed your ministry.

If you are called to ministry, you know you can't do it on your own. Let Praxis provide the companions you need to equip God's people for life in the kingdom.

www.ivpress.com/praxis